I'm Here, Now What?

A Woman's Guide in Corporate America

By

Toni Perry Gillispie

Published by

Queen V Publishing
Dayton, Ohio
QueenVPublishing.net

Published by

Queen V Publishing
Dayton, Ohio
QueenVPublishing.net
Info@PenoftheWriter.com

Copyright © 2008 by Latonia Perry Gillispie

All rights reserved. No part of this book may be reproduced or transmitted in any form or by any means, electronic or mechanical, without prior written consent of the Publisher, except for the inclusion of brief quotes in a review.

Queen V Publishing is a Christian contract publishing company of standard and integrity. We allow God's Word in you to do what it was sent to do for others.

Library of Congress Control Number: 2008936914

ISBN-13: 978-0-9817436-3-9

Cover design by Candace K
Edited by Valerie L. Coleman of PenoftheWriter.com

Printed in the United States of America

Praise for
I'm Here, Now What?...

"FINALLY! A how-to manual for women in Corporate America! While our numbers increase in the workplace, our rise to the top has yet to equal that of our male counterparts. Mrs. Perry Gillispie offers advice, counsel and real-world strategies to propel women to higher heights. Thanks, Toni, for an insider's guide to success!"
    Karen M. R. Townsend, Ph.D.
    Founder of SISTER TO SISTER: An African American Women's Think Tank

"In *I'm Here, Now What?*, Toni Perry Gillispie brings together experience and observation to craft her perspective on what it takes to be a major player in Corporate America. Her no-nonsense approach to the 'rules of engagement' offers a basic format for success that applies to women in general and women of color, in particular."
    Giselle S. Johnson, Esq.
    Chief Examiner - Civil Service Board and past president of Ohio Business and Professional Women

"Toni Perry Gillispie translates her personal style and professional ethics beautifully. To those of us who have worked in business and provided accomplishments as volunteers, *I'm Here, Now What?* is a narrative of the essential basics that support the ideal workplace citizen!"
    Julia Maxton
    Local Chamber President

Dedication

This book is dedicated to the women who have chosen a career in Corporate America.

Acknowledgements

The Power Ladies, my circle of advisors, motivated me to start writing. We have been together about seven years and meet on a regular basis to mentor and advise each other. You will learn more about them in a later chapter.

I want to thank my publisher, Valerie L. Coleman, for all of her hard work to help me meet my deadline. I do not think I could have been a published author without her guidance and assistance in completing this book.

I want to thank my family, especially my husband, Goodie, for allowing me the time to complete this book.

I want to thank my former and current employers for giving me the opportunity to learn and grow at their expense. From those experiences, I can share my challenges and successes with you.

Finally, thanks to Dr. Karen Townsend, Giselle Johnson and Julia Maxton for giving of their time to read and review the following pages. These women have been incredible sources of strength, information and role models for me and others.

I'm Here, Now What?

Table of Contents

Introduction 12
Dream 13
Emergency Plan Outline 14
Networking 17
Stress 22
Image & Brand 26
Do the Right Thing 31
Happiness Quotient 33
Oreo 35
Challenges for the Recent College Graduate 39
Challenges for Women at Forty 41
Managing Your Manager 43
Areas of Improvement 46
A Mentor 48
The A-List 50
Male-Dominated Career 52
Faith 55
Power Ladies 57
Juggling Act 61
Future Trends 65
Passion 68
Enjoy What You've Got 71
Quotes About or For Women 73
About Toni Perry Gillispie 77
Queen V Publishing 78
Pen of the Writer 80

Introduction

I'm no writer, so I'll warn you now. This book is about corporate life; more importantly, how a woman can survive in Corporate America. I pledge to share openly and honestly about my experience in the hopes that my advice can help you survive.

Your journey of finding out what to do next will not end after reading *I'm Here, Now What?* I encourage you to stay focused on not only the what, but who should be part of your passion. Get focused on yourself.

Now read and learn from my mistakes and successes. Let's peel back the onion — though it often brings tears — to discover another layer of growth, introspective knowledge and love. I have combined an array of tips, checklists and raw stories to demonstrate how a woman can use issues of spirituality, technical expertise and good old common sense to thrive in the workplace.

Toni Perry Gillispie

Dream

I dare you to dream again. When I was a little girl, I dreamed about being a dancer, teacher and then a lawyer. The reality is that at the age of forty five, I am none of the above. However, the threat of a potential layoff got my dream juices flowing again.

Don't wait for a pink slip. While you have the benefits of health insurance, company stocks and a 401k, dream again.

Complete the following sentence:

When I was a little girl, I dreamed of becoming _____, _____ or _____.

If you reached your goal in at least one of the aspirations, congratulations! You are amongst a few people who can say, "I'm living my dream." If you are not working in one of the listed careers, that is alright. Are you still interested? If so, investigate the requirements to get into your "dream" career. What do you have to lose?

During my potential layoff crisis, one of my mentors asked me if I had an emergency plan. Emergency plan? What is that?

Emergency Plan Outline

Write your plan now. Keep it simple and consider these items:
1. Affirmation statement. In the midst of a crisis, you will have to encourage yourself. For example, if I get laid off from this job, God will make a way. I am talented, gifted and smart. I will find a new career.
2. List all of your bills. Include creditors' names, addresses, balances and minimum payments. Create a payoff schedule for the most expensive debts by sorting interest rates from highest to lowest.
3. Determine the minimal earning requirements to satisfy your financial obligations for six months.
4. Start a savings plan.
5. List the names and phone numbers of twenty people who can help you find a job.
6. List ten organizations or companies for which you have volunteered. These companies are a great starting point because your reputation has already been established.
7. Investigate two to five new careers, including the "dream" careers you noted.
8. If you were to open a business, what product/service would you provide? Develop a business plan. Check with the local chamber of

commerce, community college and small business council for help.
9. File your plan in an accessible place and review it often.
10. Other pertinent activities:
    a. Attend an industry-specific trade show or meeting.
    b. Meet with mentor(s).
    c. Stay positive and surround yourself with positive people.
    d. Pray.

Now that your plan is complete, you should feel energized and free. Let's get back to dreaming.

Dreaming is important. Why? If you don't dream, you set yourself up for others, including your company, to have too much power. Never let the threat of a layoff or termination make you feel inadequate, upset and stressed.

I sat in a meeting where we were told that the company needed to reduce headcount. I thought on the worst case scenario. What if I get laid off? What about my health insurance and other benefits? How will I pay my bills? I got in my car just as the tears formed in my eyes. My worrying yielded too much power to others.

Take this same scenario and fast forward to today. My reaction would be quite different. I can work my emergency plan with emphasis on step 10d.

At times you may be on a two-track dream plan. RoNita Hawes Sanders, the first African-American woman to own and operate an urban radio station in Dayton, Ohio, said, "You may have to work your regular job to pay bills and work your dream track at the same time." It took her ten years to realize her dream. It may take you longer. The key is endurance. Even if you are in your perfect job now, things could change overnight. Be flexible and ready for change.

America needs smart women in all industry arenas. Some of us will choose to be entrepreneurs, while others will choose the non-profit arena. You have the power to pursue the arena that best fits your gifts.

You choose. The corporate life comes with long hours and in most cases, weekends. I focus my dreams on how I can advance at my current employer.

Clay Mathile, philanthropist and former owner of IAMS Pet Foods, said, "An entrepreneur is someone who chooses to work sixteen hours a day for themselves versus eight hours a day for someone else."

Dream. Let your mind and heart take you to your dream job.

Networking

Become a good networker. Notice I said "good," not great. The goal is to get started and shoot for greatness later.

In the beginning of my career, networking was difficult for me to embrace. Oftentimes, I would be the only female and person of color at the event. I dreaded the looks, sneers and sighs sprinkled between warmth, kindness and genuine friendship.

As a long-time member of a business and professional women's club, we lobbied for women's rights, established a scholarship and provided regular networking opportunities. One evening, a featured speaker gave us networking tips. She used FORM as an acronym for family, organization, responsibility and motivation. The concept was simple:

- o Family. Most everyone likes to talk about their family including their pets.
- o Organization. Many people have a sense of pride when they talk about their employer.
- o Responsibility. Who doesn't like to toot their horn about roles, duties and responsibilities?
- o Motivation. Beyond work issues, delve into personal interests: golf, music, painting, volunteering, etc. What activity makes a person tick?

She encouraged us to use it at our next networking event.

I tried it and networked with ease. Think of it like making a sandwich. The first slice of bread is a handshake, the meat is the FORM acronym, the cheese is your business card and the final slice of bread is the parting handshake.

We have been trained to give a bone-crushing handshake. Instead, match the grip of the other person. People like to feel connected to the people in their business. The handshake is one way to make a professional connection.

Share experiences as you network. The communication helps to establish a common ground or bond from which the relationship can grow. By using FORM in your conversation, you are on your way to forming business rapport.

An effective business woman is never without her cheese; the business card. Keep cards in your briefcase and car's glove compartment. Make sure that your contact information is current and indicates what you do. No one wants or has the time to guess your product or service.

Be strategic in your networking opportunities. At first, you may have to attend a lot of events. This exposure helps to establish you in the business community as an expert and contact for your company.

The final slice of bread is your parting handshake. If someone is holding you hostage with their conversation, make an expeditious, yet tactful, exit. Extend your hand, thank the person for their time and leave.

The following tips will help you on your journey to becoming a good networker:

1. Have your business cards — cheese — in hand.

2. Place your nametag on the right side for better visibility.
3. Find three people you know to begin your networking campaign. This trial run will build your confidence.
4. Use the person's name several times during the conversation. This technique helps you remember their name and builds rapport.
5. Talk, but don't dominate the conversation. Listen and learn.
6. Engage others as appropriate.
7. Make notes on the person's business card to help you remember them. Capture where and when you met and details about their FORM comments.
8. Find three people you don't know and repeat steps 4 to 7.
9. If you promise to call, by all means, call.
10. Thank the host before leaving the event.
11. After the event, send a hand-written note or email to the host and your new contacts.

Since no one likes a dry sandwich, several condiments can be added.

The first condiment to place on your sandwich is the on-factor. Upon entering a room, people know two things about you: your gender and your race.

You are not a member of the "Good Old Boys' Club" and neither should you try to be. The club is established. Some of the members allow women to participate in the club, while others do not. Either way, they do not pay your bills, although some of them may think otherwise.

Display a professional image in your attire and communication. You are "on" from the time you get to the parking lot until you leave. Be cognizant of the fact that you are being observed.

If you are a woman of color, never use or tolerate off-color jokes. You do not have to risk your career by being outspoken. Silence can be as powerful as a verbal response.

As part of the "on-factor," let me share some advice my mother gave to me: Unless you have established that all involved parties are in Las Vegas, never say anything that cannot be repeated — another essential condiment.

I attended a women's meeting that I thought was a safe environment. A month later, I received a phone call.

"This is three people removed, but someone said, that you said, that they heard from someone else..."

I knew who, what and when she talked about which goes back to being able to repeat what you say.

The other challenge is that your verbal or written comments could become the headline for the local newspaper.

As a corporate representative, your on-factor is always on. The time may come when people know you, but you do not know them. I have been at church, the bank, the day spa and had people call my name. Most of them recognized me from an event featured in the local paper or TV news media.

I'm Here, Now What?

As your brand grows, you will encounter similar responses. The recognition means that your reputation is emerging.

My dad once said, "Your reputation is all that you have. Once it's gone, it's gone; like feathers thrown in the wind."

Keep your reputation intact. Avoid going to the wrong places. Be aware of your words and actions in public. You will not be perfect, but control what you can to minimize disruptions.

Are you familiar with the Serenity Prayer? I learned it as a pledgee to a social club while in college.

God grant me the courage to change the things I can, to accept the things I cannot change and the wisdom to know the difference.
~ Author Unknown

Keep this prayer in mind as you journey through your career. Plenty of things will occur that are beyond your realm of control. Concentrate on knowing what you can change and then act on it.

Stress

Let me tell you a story about how stress impacted my career.

Five o'clock in the morning and I had to host customers in a city that was ninety minutes away. Before making the drive, I went to the office to check emails. An hour later, I left for the event. Upon arrival, I networked, talked about the company's issues and made sure my guests were happy.

At 6:00 P.M, I still had the long drive ahead of me. Did I go straight home? No. I went to the office to check emails again. About 9:00 P.M., I left the office. Ten minutes into the drive a pain hit my chest. Since it was a dull pain, I dismissed it as non-threatening. By the time I arrived home at 9:45 P.M., the pain had intensified. I called Dial-a-Nurse and was instructed to go to the hospital. The Emergency Room staff performed test after test; with no diagnosis.

The next day, I went to my doctor. I love my doctor for his honesty and openness. I sat in the waiting area and read my emails, mail and other important items. I told the doctor the story of events from the prior day.

He asked, "Why are you working so hard? Are you trying to get promoted?"

I'm Here, Now What?

His line of questioning caught me off guard. I stared at him and then tilted my head to the right. I had never thought about it.

Women are conditioned to work twice as hard as our counterparts. And for me, as a woman of color, that meant three times as hard. Why was I working so many hours?

"Hi. My name is Toni and I'm a workaholic." Do you know what that is? I buried myself in work and had nothing left for what or who really mattered.

The doctor explained my choices. "Either figure out how to make the job work or find a less stressful job."

I heard "make less money."

He ordered tests which all came back negative. His diagnosis: stress. Stress: an ugly word synonymous with heart attack, stroke, high blood pressure, nervous breakdown or aneurysm. Stress.

Some people like stress because it keeps them focused. Others learn how to live with it. Whatever your preference, get your stress level checked. Extreme stress adds no value to your life. It zaps your energy, joy and peace.

I have learned to avoid taking on the problems of others and not let someone's emergency become mine. Most of all, I am learning how to say, "No." No — a complete sentence without verb or noun.

Dealing with stress has been a long-term journey. It has taken me years to get to the point of controlling stress.

My sister programmed me on the "Just Say No" concept. At times, she had me repeat after her.

"No. See, Toni, it's easy. You say it."

"No."

Now you try it. Speak it with clarity and confidence. Keep at it. Learn to say "no" and increase your happiness quotient.

A friend of mine said that she says "no" in stages. When the request is made she replies, "Let me think about it." Once she has had time to evaluate the request — time, result needed, resources — she calls with an answer.

You have to determine if the request is significant to your career or personal interest. The key thing to remember is that you are not obligated to say "yes" to every request. Your time is precious. You get twenty four hours in a day; you decide how to spend it.

With stress comes guilt. When I found myself with nothing to do, guilt overtook me. If I had idle time after I dropped clothes to the cleaners, shopped for groceries, filled the gas tank, cleaned the house, washed clothes, read the Bible, reviewed meeting notes, finished a report, listened to music tapes for choir practice, checked in with family and called a friend, I still felt guilty. Guilt only serves to drain your creativity and ability to think clearly.

Spend time by yourself. If I knew in my twenties what I know now, a few years later, I would have enjoyed more ME time. As women, we tend to give to others without restraint and forget to give to ourselves.

Make a commitment to yourself and complete this sentence:

I'm Here, Now What?

Beginning today, I commit to spend more time with me doing _____ or _____.

I attended the Sister to Sister Conference where we received a list of self-pampering items. The suggested activities revived me because most of them were free or of little cost.

- Brush your teeth by candlelight.
- Sit in your yard and let the sun hit your face.
- Read your favorite book.
- Take a bubble bath.
- Take a guilt-free nap.
- Enjoy a picnic meal in the park.
- Call an old friend.
- Put your favorite photos in an album.
- Take a ride to no where in particular and then stop for a meal.
- Listen to music.
- Write your burdens, feelings and issues in a journal.

Create a list of your favorite things to do by and for yourself. I often think about a massage, but never seem to make time for it. Stop thinking and do it. Time is going to pass either way. Get involved in an activity that you have always wanted or needed for yourself. Do it today.

A few of my favorite things…

_____

_____

_____

_____

Image & Brand

Every time you walk into a room or your name is mentioned in business circles, it evokes a feeling, emotion or thought. How do people respond to your name?

Someone who cared about me and my future gave me the following advice:

"Toni, keep doing what you're doing. Become good at it. Be comfortable with who you are. Believe in yourself."

Restate his advice, but personalize it by substituting your name for mine.

When I first heard these words, it was like hearing music, but not understanding the lyrics. Several spins later, I got the meaning of the message.

You have an image that is communicated in three levels: physical, verbal and written.

Physical

Designer clothes are not a prerequisite to be well groomed. It is ludicrous to buy top-of-the-line clothes on an entry-level salary. Opt to buy classic pieces that work together and flow from day meetings to evening receptions.

In the business arena, men may have to get comfortable seeing a woman in leadership. After consistent appearances, they will begin to acknowledge you as a professional. Once you demonstrate your expertise, they will come to trust you.

Maintain a high standard of grooming, even on business-casual day. I worked for a company that showed new hires a film on acceptable attire. The film demonstrated fabrics, appropriate skirt lengths, hair styles and jewelry. After viewing the film, I felt my image was lacking because I wore glasses, my hair was long and I did not own a gold watch.

Look for good examples at your company. Observe the women at staff meetings, community dinners, etc. Do not be discouraged by sneers when you enter a room. Your goal is to listen, look and learn. Take a physical inventory of yourself. Look at your nails. Are they clean, the proper length and polished with a conservative color? Is your hair frizzy, too long or damaged? Are your shoes shined with the heel intact? Your hygiene must never come into question.

I went to an event featuring a high-level woman manager from a local company. Her outfit was wrinkled; her feet and hands were dusty. Her appearance was a distraction to her message.

No excuses. If you only have four suits and two shirts, then rotate them. Keep them pressed and cleaned. You want people to focus on your message and not how you look. A successful woman wears proper-fitting clothes, with limited jewelry, makeup and cologne. She understands the power of looking right and having a professional physical image.

Verbal

What about your verbal image; the spoken word? Slang and Ebonics have no place in the board room or the work environment. If you want to slow your upward mobility, use profanity. Try these helpful hints:

1. Companies demand strong verbal and written presentation skills.
2. Practice articulating your thoughts in two minutes or less. A Toastmaster Club can be a great resource to hone your oratory skills. The group provides a safe environment to practice and improve your speaking prowess.
3. Review notes prior to meetings to formulate questions or observations.
4. Speak in clear, concise sentences.
5. Do not monopolize the conversation.
6. Do not try to sound intelligent, rather be intelligent. Become an expert in your field.

An effective leader has to think clearly and speak well to be taken seriously and offer valuable ideas.

Written

Emails, reports and reimbursement requests, can be used by management to move you up or out of a company. Consider these writing tips:

1. Write, edit and spell check your work. Do not rely on your computer to catch grammatical errors. For example, you typed "he" and meant to type "the."
2. Never write and send an email in anger. Recall trying to gather those feathers that have been thrown into the wind. It cannot be done. Write

a draft and then discuss it with your mentor or hold until you are no longer angry.
3. Only carbon copy (cc) the appropriate managers and team members.
4. Do not fight an issue in email, letters or any other written form. Articulate your business case, written or verbally, and then call a meeting or conference call to discuss it further. The impersonal nature of emails can distort the message. Since you cannot couple the words with nonverbal cues like facial expressions, gestures and voice inflections, the full intent of the communication can be lost.
5. Take the high road and allow others a way out. If a team member does not want to participate in a process, allow them to explain their position and bow out.
6. State who, what, why, where and how in your business case.
7. Be succinct. Do not over write.

Your image can grow or sink your career. You are a brand and your image must add value to your brand.

Brand names like Starbucks, Target or Mercedes create thoughts and feelings about the companies and their offerings; strong coffee, good buys and quality cars, respectively. I want people to perceive me as a viable resource. If I commit to calling them, then I call. If I do not know an answer, then I tell the truth.

Develop and protect your brand. Don't be like some politicians or sales people who say and do anything to get your buy-in. Be strategic. Be authentic. Be yourself.

A politician told me that she was not a politician, but someone who happened to be in politics. A difference exists and perception is everything.

Your personal brand is powerful as it speaks volumes to your credibility and ability.

Marianne Williamson said, "The great part is that the power is not just in some of us; it is in all of us."

You have power. Power to set forth a brand that says you are a professional expert. You are not a politician, but someone who happens to be in politics. Does your employer see the value in your brand?

You probably never thought that you are a brand. Some may even say that you are putting a label on me. Yes, that's correct. Either you determine how people will think, feel and see you or they will create their own reality.

Complete this sentence:

When my name, [put your name here], is called, I want the business community to _____ (feel), _____ (see) and _____ (think) about me and my work.

Knowing that you are a brand can help determine the steps needed to grow, nurture and protect your image. Do the right thing.

Do the Right Thing

Spike Lee wrote the movie, *Do the Right Thing* which focused on relationships. Business is relation driven. If you do the right thing in your relationships, then you are on your way to success.

Doing the right thing includes saying what you mean since unethical behavior will destroy your brand. In fact, it could damage you and your company. Familiarize yourself with the company's code of ethics — designed to help you do the right thing in the workplace. It may provide instruction on what to do if you get a gift, receive confidential information or observe unethical behavior.

I previously mentioned that you do not want to say or do anything that could be picked up as a headline in the local news. You also do not what to be the subject of negative conversation between your boss and/or upper management.

On one occasion, I sought support on a company issue from a local leader. I sent the person general information via a confidential email and then called to request a meeting. The person denied the meeting and became upset over the issue. He sent me a scathing email with copies to the Statehouse.

Why am I sharing this experience with you? I did the right thing by asking for support however the person I tried to engage did something unethical, in my opinion. Since he denied the face-to-face meeting, without having all of the facts, he sent an erroneous message to key officials.

You cannot control another person's behavior. You can only control your response. If you find yourself in a similar situation, put together your reaction strategy. When developing your strategy, consider the following:

1. How will you respond to the person who initiated the situation? Via email or phone call? Do you apologize although you have done nothing wrong?
2. Who within your organization needs to know of the issue?
3. What is the protocol for making a mistake public?
4. What, if any, response needs to be made to people outside the organization who have been drawn into the issue?
5. When you see the external people, do you mention the deed?

Take the high road. I should have limited the information contained in the email. I should have anticipated his response. I should not have... No need to dwell on the issue. A sent email becomes available for others to read; a permanent record. Know the person you are contacting and use your instincts to determine whether they are someone you can trust.

Know the people you think would be willing to help. Surround yourself with people who want the company to be successful and have a genuine interest in your success. Developing good business relationships requires time and reciprocity.

Happiness Quotient

Happiness is fleeting. I have had moments of happiness and minutes of happiness. Happiness at work is a flawed act.

> *We do not live to work. We work to live.*
> ~ Author Unknown

If you start living for your job, you will only find temporary happiness. Happiness is not what one should seek anyway. Consider a new approach to work. Seek activities you enjoy because joy has staying power. Let's say that you got passed over for a promotion; joy remains. If your annual review was a complete surprise because your rating was lower than expected, joy can still remain. Seek joy and find stability. It is the voice inside you that says, "I am smart. I have skills. I will land on my feet in a better situation." You are all of these things and more.

Joy keeps you believing in yourself. Joy helps you to be comfortable with who you are and what you have to offer. You bring great value to the company, but you can offer more to your family through activities that bring you joy.

Happiness, on the other hand, comes and goes. If you are unhappy, you may believe that you are not qualified for your job and question your skills and abilities. Joy gets you up in the morning, takes you through the workday and brings you home with a smile. If you hold true to the axiom that you work to live, then you will find joy in being there. This internal pleasure will result in increased productivity, reduced stress and balance in your life.

With joy, you can look forward to the evening and time with family, friends or alone. Joy helps you remember that the company pays your salary, but does not own you.

Find balance in your life. I have tried for twenty years to find balance with no success. Nurture a lifestyle that gives you sufficient ME time and family time. Take control of your schedule. If not, it will take control of you.

You will have days when you say to yourself, "I cannot believe that I get paid to do this job." Other days you may feel that the company under pays you. In either case, seek joy, not happiness. Joy will find the hope to go another day. You will not always walk on a bed of flowered ease, but during the dry season, joy can sustain you.

Oreo

A negative connotation is attached to the word "Oreo." Black on the outside and white on the inside meant that an African-American person was "acting White."

A potential trap for a woman of color working in a Caucasian environment is the I-am-one-of-them syndrome. Be yourself. Do not pretend to be someone for the sake of acceptance. Some people will deal with you only because of whom you represent, while others will fully embrace you and establish relationships that become friendships.

I never considered my relationship skills as a gift until I spoke with a professor. She said that the ability to successfully work in a male-dominated arena as a woman of color is a gift. A gift? Your goal should be to relate to all races, economic backgrounds and social levels.

One day, as I waited for an event I began a conversation with the security guard. He was the brother of a prominent local preacher and a retiree of the company for which I worked.

Another example is that I used to sell men's clothing. A gentleman wearing a three-piece suit came into the store. I assumed that he had money and would buy from me. He did not. The next day, a man in a jogging suit and gym shoes came into the store and purchased three suits, shirts and ties to match. The lesson: never judge a book by its cover.

One way to learn about your company is to listen to everyone from the janitor to the human resources manager. Treat everyone with respect and you will get respect in return. A good manager does not have to tell people that she is the manager.

I attended a business function where I was seated with strangers. I spoke with everyone at the table. I spent extra time with the people on each side of me. After the event, the gentleman to my right, president of a local company, gave me his card. He encouraged me to call him if he could be of service.

One year later, I purchased my first home and arranged to turn on the gas. Moving day and no gas. I called customer service and was shuffled through several representatives. After being on hold for fifteen minutes, the representative said that I needed to do what I had to do. Since it was Friday afternoon, I would not get gas until Monday.

I found the contact information for the gentleman I ate lunch with months prior. I called and explained to him how I had been treated. In one hour, I had service.

During your career, you will have to deal with stupid; not stupid people, but stupid actions. You still have to uphold a standard of professionalism.

Regardless of your ethnicity, people like to be treated with respect. We are all one race; the human race. Everyone wants good schools, a nice neighborhood and a job to pay their bills. Your job is to exalt others and then you will be exalted. Seek those people who desire to transition their people to the next level. Be a person to help versus hinder. You will experience success that cannot be taken away.

I'm Here, Now What?

A gift? You need to be who you are. If you happen to be in a male-dominated arena and are making it work, wonderful. If you are having trouble, then examine yourself. Ask for help if necessary. Learn the written and unwritten rules of the trade. If all else fails, try another career. You have the power to control yourself and respond in a positive manner.

Know your strengths and weaknesses and don't let others define you. Capitalize on your strengths. Make your weaknesses opportunities for improvement through personal development or by surrounding yourself with people who can fill the gap.

I worked in an area that I knew well. I focused on my strengths of meeting facilitation, follow-up and overall business knowledge and stopped beating myself up over what I did not know. I let the people around me fill the gap until I was proficient.

Life is a continuous learning process. I read journals, articles and papers. I listen to CNN, NPR, Rush Limbaugh — yes, Rush — and other thought-provoking leaders.

Oreo does not have to have a negative connotation attached to it. Understanding how people think helps you relate to them, and in relating, you learn how to manage them. I use this process of understanding to gain knowledge about the community, my profession and people. An Oreo, therefore, is someone with the ability to relate to all kinds of people — speak the right language, to the right people, at the right time. Mastering this skill will result in the gift of relationship; sincere relationships with reciprocal benefits that can advance your career. Be authentic. Rise above the Oreo mentality. The competitive nature of Corporate America requires you to differentiate yourself from others. Let your interpersonal and relational skills be distinguishing qualities and execute your job with greatness.

Consider the following components of relating:
1. Gain command of the King's English.
2. Learn how to speak the person's language by listening to what is important to them.
3. Be knowledgeable in a plethora of topics including sports, music and books.
4. Be who you are so people can come to know what is important to you.

I'm Here, Now What?

Challenges for the Recent College Graduate

After four years of college and one year as a co-op student, I prepared for graduation. No job prospects, plenty of debt and no one to talk me through the transition. The interviews had not gone well. My skills did not match the job requirements because I did not have enough computer, accounting or work experience.

I followed the formula — college + good grades + hard work = good employment — but an important variable was missing.

Getting a job is not always about qualifications or a great resume. Sometimes it is about who you know. If you want to expedite the job search process, prior to graduation, consider these things:

Network with your professors and administrators. Many have worked in other industries before joining the university. They can provide you with referrals and references.

Volunteer in your field of study. Volunteering places you inside of an organization and affords access to decision makers. Ask for a meeting with the president, volunteer coordinator and/or department manager of interest. Develop four to five questions about their line of work, how they entered the field, advice they have for you and then ask for a referral.

Read, read and read. You can gain expert knowledge by reading industry journals. These magazines list job opportunities and websites that can be used for further research.

List your top three industry preferences, for example, banking, insurance and accounting firms. Under each category, identify companies of interest by city. Prioritize the three industries taking into consideration location, living expenses and correlation to ultimate career objectives. Start your job search with the top-ranking company. Call or check their website for information and job postings. If the company has an intern or job shadow program, the opportunity will add value to your experience and resume.

Challenges for Women at Forty

At one point in my career, recruiters called me for job opportunities and referrals. Not anymore.

When you reach forty years old, some consider you either too experienced to be affordable or over qualified. As the employment base grows older and the need for skilled workers increases, a slight shift in this school of thought has occurred.

Be good at what you do. You can be more strategic in your volunteer choices. Pass on your knowledge as a mentor to someone within or outside of your organization. At this juncture, you have two options to consider: ride the wave to retirement or strive for a promotion. The latter can be promotion within the company or a career change. For either option, try the following steps:

1. Determine the next job move.
2. Determine who can help you get there, internal and external to the company.
3. Develop your plan of action.
4. In the words of Nike, "Just do it."

Based on national statistics, at forty, you have lived over half of your projected life span. Redeem time now. I started writing this book in 2001. Seven years later, I put my thoughts on paper. Your biggest challenge is to do what you have always wanted to do. Start today!

What creeps along and is simultaneously as fast as lighting? TIME. Time shows on your hands, face and waistline. Time snatched your college figure.

I asked myself, "When are you going to start enjoying life's gifts?" I have always wanted to dance in Paris, draw, play piano and learn to speak Spanish.

In my twenties, my phone rang several times a year with new opportunities. In my thirties, I worked in two major cities. In my forties, my phone stopped ringing.

The time is now. Don't wait for the alarm clock of life to wake you at eighty. Wake up!

I'm Here, Now What?

Managing Your Manager

Managing your manager is an art. Here are few questions you need to answer:
1. What is his/her management style? Micro, hands off or somewhere in between?
2. How does he/she prefer to communicate? Email, phone or face-to-face?
3. How does he/she view your strengths? Weaknesses?
4. Is he/she your boss, mentor or a combination? If not a mentor, who can you ask in or outside of your organization to mentor you?
5. How does his/her style mesh with yours?

During my banking career, I experienced the hands-on, or micro, manager. He rifled through my in-box and prioritized my work. He made frequent requests for verbal reports on what I was doing and with whom I worked. His demands reminded me of the "who's-on-first-what's-on-second" routine. His micro-management style drove me crazy. On the other end of the continuum, is the hands-off manager.

Some folks believe that the liberty is a blessing. Oh, to have your manager absent from daily operations. Do not be fooled by this style. Out of sight is not out of mind.

You are on a continuous cycle of review, study and observation. What should you do? Manage your manager. If he/she does not communicate with you, then it is your job to initiate communication. Send regular updates on your activities by voice mail or email. If your manager decides not to accept your updates, then log your activities. Attach numerical values to quantify your value to the company. For example, percent improved, dollars saved and increased revenue.

An eyeball moment with your manager is critical. Request a monthly or quarterly face-to-face meeting to make sure you are on the right track. If you are given specific advice or recommendations for improvement, capture it in your journal. Incorporate the advice into your daily routine and keep it in your file.

Network with your peers to check and compare notes. Be mindful that not everyone will give you input or assistance. After three to six months, you should know who you can trust to help you and in turn who you can help. Remember even the person you value the most will not share everything.

Staff meetings are opportunities to network with your boss, peers, presenters and upper management.

1. Arrive a few minutes before the meeting.
2. Review the agenda.
3. If you did not receive advanced notice, retrieve any documents you need to have in the meeting.
4. Develop one to three pertinent questions for the presenter.
5. Ask for his/her business card and then place it in your resource file.
6. Send thank-you notes or emails to the presenters.

A good note dropper leaves a favorable impression. I have had many networking contacts acknowledge

I'm Here, Now What?

that they received a note from me. If a disconnect between you and your boss exists, then you have two choices: Dust off your resume and start looking for another job, internal or external to the company. Success in your position is contingent upon managing your manager. Your second choice is to take charge. As a talented, smart and creative woman, study your boss. Talk to his assistant. What is important to him? What activities does he love? Where did he work before his current position?

When I got married I was told that communication is the key to a successful relationship. The same is true in the relationship you have with your boss.

I know that voicemail is an acceptable form of communication for some managers, but I did not like to receive correction or behavior coaching by voicemail — too impersonal. As a manager, I never left voicemails to correct employee behavior. Everyone is different.

Identify your manager's preferred method of communication within the first two to three months and utilize it to your benefit. The way you communicate is a direct reflection on you as it exudes power or non-professionalism. It shapes how you are viewed throughout your organization. Script your voicemail messages. Draft, read and re-read your emails and letters. The recipient could share it with his boss.

Leave nothing to chance. Once an impression is shaped it is difficult to change. Guide your manager's perception of you. He will come to value you and your skills.

Areas of Improvement

So your boss thinks you need to improve aspects of your work. Do not take it personally. Acknowledge your strengths and areas of improvement. Know when to toot your horn and when to give encouragement, or kudos, to others.

When I joined a new company, I had a few things going against my success. I was a woman in a male-dominated arena. I was hired from outside of the company and I did not know the industry. My job was to influence purchasing managers, in another city, to use minorities and women in the procurement process.

I traveled to that city and worked in the department. I attended staff meetings, vendor reviews and management trainings. I stopped focusing on what I did not know and focused on what I did know. I did not know the purchasing managers or vendors, but I learned the needs and wants of both parties. I did not know the industry, but I knew meeting facilitation and follow up.

Focus on your strengths and you can be successful. Two years into that job, I received an "exceed expectations" on my review. The following year, I took a new job. I worked tirelessly to learn the job and match the contributions of my peers. At the end of the year, I received a "does not meet expectations" on my review — a devastating low point in my career. I had never received such a rating.

I'm Here, Now What?

What is put on paper about you may or may not reflect who you are and what you deliver. Corporate America is like playing in a game. The rules may change. Your location may change. Your bosses may change. You, on the other hand, cannot change. Your core values and who you are need to remain constant. The only changes you need to make to be successful are:
1. Listen to your boss' recommendations for improvement. Do not take the information personally.
2. Ask for examples on how you can change a behavior.
3. Request a monthly/quarterly review of your progress so that you can make adjustments before the next performance evaluation.
4. Ask to be paired with or mentored by an exemplary employee.
5. Listen with the intent to learn from the review. Do little talking.
6. Do not play the self-doubt game. You are smart or you would not be there.
7. You will make mistakes, learn from them.
8. Unplug your emotions. Never cry or yell in a review or meeting. If you cannot contain yourself, ask to be excused. Go to the restroom, get it out and then return.

Make a list of the areas of deficiency and then ask for help. Do not dwell on the shortcomings, but rather make a commitment to improve them.

A Mentor

Your next step is to determine if your boss can be your mentor. If he/she can, then you are in for a much smoother journey. Otherwise, look internally or externally for someone you can trust.

A mentor is defined as a person who has traveled down the road you are on, kept the roadmap and in turn shares it with you. A mentor is concerned about your growth and offers valuable advice.

During my career, I have had both female and male mentors. The key to a successful mentor/mentee relationship is trust. Recall the days when neighbors talked at the fence. Although the conservation may have been confidential, once the two parted, word of their discussion traveled around the block. Trust takes time to develop, as will the relationship with your mentor. Until you reach the trust threshold, keep in mind that whatever you say may be repeated.

When you receive feedback or criticism, keep your mouth shut and listen. It may hurt to hear the truth, but iron sharpens iron. You have the final decision on what information to use, discard and file.

My boss called to warn me about my non-traditional speaking style. He admonished me to be more traditional in my next presentation. I took his advice as a criticism for being different; I am different. I can follow protocol with the best of them. I can also add my own flavor as needed. At first, I was offended by the observation because he was not in attendance at the

referenced event. What did I do? I filed the information for future consideration. Every time I get up to speak, I think:
1. Who is my audience?
2. What is my message?
3. How can I best help them relate to the message, not me?

Complete the following sentences:

I will ask for help on _____ by _____ (date).

I commit to making changes in my _____ and _____.

I will seek input from my boss by _____ (date).

Now read and commit to the following:

I will value my differences and use them to benefit the company.

I will list my area(s) of improvement, but will not dwell on them.

I will develop a plan of action to improve my skills today.

The A-List

Upper management passed down an edict that all managers had to participate in time management training. What did upper management think we had been doing with our time for the past year? I wrestled with the notion of needing the training. However, open to new information, I attended the class and learned that everything is not an "A."

An "A" item is defined as a priority; something that has to be done now. The system outlined how to prioritize daily activities by estimating the time to complete each task.

As I made my list, I noticed a terrible pattern: five of six tasks were "A" priority. Worse yet was that to complete the five tasks, I needed to work twelve hours that day. Did you just have a light bulb or aha moment? Everything cannot be an "A." If you are working twelve-hour days, six days a week, you have nothing to lose by trying the tips outlined below:

1. Decide how many hours you will work daily and then move past the guilt.
2. Have fun with your work. Humor can make the day move along.
3. Reflect on your successes. Build on your mistakes.
4. Love yourself more than your work.
5. Make a date with your family, friends, significant other and yourself.

I'm Here, Now What?

I think I contracted workaholic-ism while I was single; a lonely perfectionist. Just out of college, trying to climb the corporate ladder, I fell into the easy routine of work, work and work.

During my second job out of college, I left in the mornings with my mom and sisters in their pajamas. When I returned at night, they were in their pajamas. My boss felt it was important for me to get involved in the community, so I joined a committee and attended events. I spiraled out of control. Summer melted into fall. Fall merged into winter. Winter splashed into spring. Between seasons, I was in wrong relationships, including the one with myself. It just became natural to stay busy and never take time to be with me.

As a Christian, I was raised to prioritize my life as:
1. God
2. Family
3. Career

I did not realize that I needed to add myself to this list or that the order could shift. No reason existed for me to feel guilty about changing priorities or adding time in for myself. Guilt can stifle your ability to move forward and weigh you down until you believe that it is okay to stop, sit and do nothing. Guilt. It made me put everything and everybody ahead of my own well being. Learn from my mistake and avoid the guilt. Determine what is important to you — relationships, self-pampering, etc. —and then enjoy it.

Male-Dominated Career

If you happen to be in a male-dominated career, get ready for a roller coaster ride. When I graduated from college, I decided to use my nickname for business. Why? My nickname is masculine. Most of the time it worked out great, especially as a bank manager. If only I had a quarter for every person that wanted the man in charge. It was fun to explain to the customer that I was that man.

I admit that I did not care for the mail that came addressed to me as "Mr.," but twenty-five years later, I am over being taken for a man. I chock the suffix up to the sender not knowing me.

I do not have a definitive reason as to why I ended up in male-dominated positions for most of my career. Although the Good Old Boys' Club is all around you, do not try to become a member. If by chance you happen to get an invitation to a club event, remember you are a guest.

I attended an overnight conference with twice as many men as women in attendance. As we waited for the dinner event to begin, we gathered near the bar.

~ ~ ~ ~ ~ ~ ~

Sidebar: Limit alcohol at business functions.

~ ~ ~ ~ ~ ~ ~

One of the conference attendees paid for everyone's drinks and then a second round was offered. I placed the glass on the table. When it was time to go to the dinner, one of the men asked me to go with him to his room. For some unknown reason, he needed my assistance to get his business cards. I realized that he thought that I was drunk or willing to go to his room. I told him that I would meet the group downstairs.

As a professional and expert in your field, do not let down your guard. You are a woman first. If you show weakness or allow yourself to be put in a situation of vulnerability, then you could wind up in a compromising position.

I attended an event and was the only woman of color. Greeted by stares, I took my seat at the dinner table. Men were seated on either side of me. They held a lively conversation, but ignored me during the dinner. I listened. One man spoke of being a Marine who fought in World War I and the Korean War. The other spoke of a similar experience. I interjected that both my uncles were Vietnam veterans and how the war impacted them.

The gentlemen looked at me and then returned to their conversation. The topic shifted to local events. I interjected about my company's gift to a local non-profit organization and our commitment to the city.

They both smiled and one asked me a question.

It may take time to get involved or to even be accepted. If they had not acknowledged my second attempt to add to the conversation, I may have remained quiet for the rest of the dinner. That would have been fine, too.

My final attempt would have been to talk about sports. If you know a little about sports, then you can break the ice with others, especially men.

Over time, you will learn how to relate to the male bosses and stakeholders in your community.

Understand that you may or may not be embraced by them.

Think of a scenario where you are the only woman or woman of color in a room full of people.

1. What will you do to knock them dead?
2. What lesson can you learn from the event where you feel you are not welcomed?
3. How can you prepare for the next incident?
4. Do you need to replenish or reward yourself for jumping right in? For accepting the situation? For changing things around?

I went to another event and peeked into the room. I should have seen my next supporter, my next success or a new contact, but I saw that I would be the only woman of color. As an executive, you will have to decide where you spend your time and talent. Listen to your mind and heart. If your energy level is low, then you may need to replenish or reward yourself. Replenishing yourself means taking time off from work. Sleep until noon. Go to the beach. Rewarding yourself may include scheduling a manicure, brushing your teeth by candlelight or eating your favorite meal.

Fill in the blanks:

I will replenish myself by doing _____ by _____ (date).

I will reward myself by doing _____ by _____ (date).

I'm Here, Now What?

Faith

Christmas Eve 1999, the doctor called to tell the family that my mother had breast cancer. How could she have this deadly disease when she never drank or smoked? Why would God affect a noble woman who works for the good of her family?

That holiday season was difficult. We realized that the best gifts do not come from the store. Being together as a family is an amazing gift.

As I drove home to Indiana, I prayed. I needed to be in Ohio to help my family. I needed to be in a position of flexibility, but how?

The next day, while at work, the phone rang. The vice president of a company asked me if I wanted to interview for a new position in Ohio.

I am a woman of faith who believes in God and miracles. Being asked to interview for a job — a promotion, nonetheless — with the flexibility I needed was a miracle. The story behind this story is that I had interviewed for the position two years earlier, but did not receive an offer. Believing that I was qualified, disappointment settled in my heart. A short time later, I accepted another job; preparation for what God ultimately had for me. I interviewed for the Ohio position and accepted their offer for employment.

Understand that this miracle did not come overnight. I took my six and nine-month career plans into interviews with me. I also had references, resumes and qualifications. With mock interviews, documentation and perseverance, I still received numerous rejections because it was not my time to be in those jobs. Even the most qualified applicant can become frustrated after hearing, "Sorry, but you're not what we're looking for," enough times. Devastated, my ego and self esteem plummeted. I learned that ego has no place in a job search. Securing a job involves skill and politics. I took several rounds of interviews before I realized the formula depended upon more than just my qualifications. My perception shifted to reality. I was not in control.

Know that you will have to put forth a considerable amount of time and energy on your job search. Also know that in trying with all your might, for the best results, leave control in God's hands. He answered my prayer to go home and I am grateful that His blessing was based on what I needed.

Faith

Christmas Eve 1999, the doctor called to tell the family that my mother had breast cancer. How could she have this deadly disease when she never drank or smoked? Why would God affect a noble woman who works for the good of her family?

That holiday season was difficult. We realized that the best gifts do not come from the store. Being together as a family is an amazing gift.

As I drove home to Indiana, I prayed. I needed to be in Ohio to help my family. I needed to be in a position of flexibility, but how?

The next day, while at work, the phone rang. The vice president of a company asked me if I wanted to interview for a new position in Ohio.

I am a woman of faith who believes in God and miracles. Being asked to interview for a job — a promotion, nonetheless — with the flexibility I needed was a miracle. The story behind this story is that I had interviewed for the position two years earlier, but did not receive an offer. Believing that I was qualified, disappointment settled in my heart. A short time later, I accepted another job; preparation for what God ultimately had for me. I interviewed for the Ohio position and accepted their offer for employment.

Understand that this miracle did not come overnight. I took my six and nine-month career plans into interviews with me. I also had references, resumes and qualifications. With mock interviews, documentation and perseverance, I still received numerous rejections because it was not my time to be in those jobs. Even the most qualified applicant can become frustrated after hearing, "Sorry, but you're not what we're looking for," enough times. Devastated, my ego and self esteem plummeted. I learned that ego has no place in a job search. Securing a job involves skill and politics. I took several rounds of interviews before I realized the formula depended upon more than just my qualifications. My perception shifted to reality. I was not in control.

Know that you will have to put forth a considerable amount of time and energy on your job search. Also know that in trying with all your might, for the best results, leave control in God's hands. He answered my prayer to go home and I am grateful that His blessing was based on what I needed.

I'm Here, Now What?

Power Ladies

The Power Ladies is comprised of seven women who are entrepreneurs, doctoral students and high-level corporate executives. They are my circle with whom I can be me, both weak and strong.

As you grow in your career, weakness is not an option. Every woman in Corporate America needs a mentor and a circle of friends. Why? Because as you progress up the ladder, you need people who will advise, correct and console you.

The circle of friends allows you to be you only after trust has been fully established. You have probably heard the saying, "What goes on in Vegas, stays in Vegas." Your circle must be a safe haven; a confidential environment of friendship and sharing.

The Power Ladies started with my best friend who relocated to Atlanta. She needed a circle of like-minded women who related to her experiences. Her initial attempts to establish a group failed. Realizing that some of her closest friends lived in Dayton, Ohio, we decided to each invite a friend to dinner. We chose to be informally organized — no president or secretary — with a firm and formal commitment to confidentiality.

A few members have left the Power Ladies for various reasons. The current circle has been challenged due to logistics. What has not changed is the bond of respect and genuine care for each other. We have spent time listening, holding and praying for each other. We hope to keep this spirit of exhorting for years to come as we have transformed into a group who knows the value of true friendship.

The circle has arrived at this point because:
1. Each Power Lady is a star in her own career. We do not compete with each other.
2. Each Power Lady exercises confidentiality in our activities.
3. Each Power Lady wants to see the others succeed.
4. Each Power Lady offers advice in a caring, non-judgmental way.
5. Each Power Lady brings experience with her advice.
6. Each Power Lady holds the others accountable for tasks, plan adjustments and the successful completion of projects.

Although I have male mentors, a special bond exists with the Power Ladies. These women have been a source of strength and wisdom for me. We meet quarterly to afford us time to manage our home life, school and career. My greatest joy is that I can call or email any one of the Power Ladies for help.

A few careers back, as executive director, I oversaw the launch of a new federal program. Because of unrealistic goals, the program got off to a rocky start. Unable to get the goals changed, I built upon the strengths of the program. We sailed along, until disaster struck.

The front page of the local paper featured a negative story about one of the program's participants. She had received a loan and left town without a trace. Seated in my office, I cried without restraint.

I'm Here, Now What?

A female leader called to see how I was taking the news. After she realized that I was upset and confused, she came to my office. We left the building, went for a drive and I cried on her shoulder.

As I regained my composure, she asked, "What is your plan?"

I paused. I had no plan. In fact, I had considered leaving the program however she guided me through a plan that gave me hope. Instead of running away, her questions re-energized me. I wanted to get back to the office to implement the plan.

Although she was not a Power Lady, she was my power at that time. No one knew that I was in my office crying. I could not let my employees or board members see me in disarray. They looked to me for answers and strength. I just needed time to fill my cup so I could in turn fill theirs.

Whether you have an established group like the Power Ladies or a mentor/friend like the power woman who came to my rescue, you need someone. We cannot do it alone. We need people in our corner who want us to be successful. In an hour of need, who will you call for advice or a shoulder to lean on? As a woman in Corporate America, you need to figure out who before you need them.

Were there days when I should have talked to a Power Lady or powerful woman to ask for advice? Yes. Were there times when I wished I had talked the problem over with one of them? Yes.

You may or may not take advantage of the special relationships, however if it is available, save yourself some heartache and make the call. Everyone is not blessed with a confidant or trustworthy friend. It takes time, but in the end the value of your circle will be priceless.

I encourage you to start your own power circle. You will be glad that you did.

fictitious. You cannot mimic her supernatural abilities all of the time. Even Super Woman needs time off from bringing order to a chaotic world. If you lose your health, mind or ability to help others, then what?

Do you suffer from the if-I-don't-do-it-then-it-won't-get-done syndrome? Trust me, it may take a little longer, but if it's important, then it will get done. If it does not get completed, life continues. Learn how to live your life in a way that brings you joy and then joy to others.

I once thought that things could not run without me. Get sick or care for someone who is sick, and you will see that life can go on. How? You shift priorities and focus on the important matters: family and self-preservation. You will come to know the precious nature of your life and the lives of those you love.

Dr. Karen Townsend gave me a great example of taking care of you. She said that before the plane departs, the flight attendant says, "In the unlikely event of a decrease in cabin pressure, an oxygen mask will drop from the overhead compartment. Place your mask on first and then assist others." Think about it. If you pass out, who will put masks on your children or others needing assistance?

Welcome to life; the life of the woman with two full-time jobs: one at home and one at work. Overwhelmed? Expect and accept it. Burned the toast on occasion? Scrape it off or try again or no bread with breakfast. If you are a woman in Corporate America, then develop a plan that will help you be successful at home.

What other tips will help your home success plan?
1. Give the children tasks.

2. Require everyone to clean up their own mess.
3. Do not overbook the family schedule.
4. Learn to say, "No."
5. _____
6. _____
7. _____

Your job is unending however you have the power to make changes that benefit you and your family. Use the tips above to remove clutter and bring clarity to your schedule. Your time is precious. Make the best of it for yourself, your family and your community. Be strategic and remember that "No" is a complete sentence. No sense juggling your life into a stressful mess.

Use your gifts and talents to create peace. During our wedding ceremony, my husband promised that our home would be a place of peace. Our home is my sanctuary.

Create a space that is yours. Create time that is yours. You will lose your mind if you juggle all of the balls without relief. Understand that you will have days when the balls keep coming. I have sat my desk for hours only to look at the clock and realize that I am late —real late — getting home. I could stay at my office twenty-four hours and not read every email or return every call. When I die, I do not want my tombstone to read, "I wish I had spent more time at the office." I want it to read, "I enjoyed my life. I shared my life. I loved my life."

Future Trends

I work for a company that invests heavily in forward thinking. Given the competitive nature of the industry and the savvy of our customers, we have to plan ahead. Our customers help shape legislative, regulatory and community focus for the company. The customer is the boss and without vision, the company would die.

The same is true of your career. You may be good at what you do, but you have to look at what lies ahead. For example, the local news reported that numerous manufacturing jobs were leaving the city. The employees were offered severance packages or pink slips. The trend of layoffs and plant closings should have triggered a wave of proactive re-training or entrepreneurs. However many workers were second and third-generation factory employees and believed that a layoff was unlikely. They showed up to work and delivered a quality product, until it hit the fan, so to speak.

The plant is gone. The market is shrinking. The quality of life has impacted the community. I am blessed to have two degrees and experience in banking, economic development, supplier diversity and community affairs. If anything should happen to my current job, then I would rely on my education, skills and faith to jumpstart my next career.

Why spend time discussing future trends? First, my skills are from the past. We must not dwell on the past, but look to the future. Employment trends call for strategic thinking, presentation skills and proficiency in technology. I cannot rely on my past experiences to get or keep me in a successful career.

Second, company loyalty to employees is minimal. Back in the day — that's so cliché —one could graduate from high school and get a blue-collar job that placed them in the middle class. Not so today. I tell young people that they must earn at least an associates degree or trade. Without a degree, you probably will not be hired into Corporate America.

Finally, a woman needs to have credentials. You will produce credibility as an expert, if you have a degree, experience and knowledge. Make a commitment to keep learning. Make a commitment to get exposure and increase your brand (see *Networking* and *Image & Brand*). No excuses.

If you are current on industry trends, then you can anticipate what is next. You can get information from the Internet, trade magazines, your internal and external contacts and your boss. Review the articles and employee emails. I know; we tend to erase them, but I encourage you to take a look at them. You could miss vital details that could enhance your career or give you futuristic information.

We can get so caught up in meeting deadlines and daily issues that we forget about the future. Every decision we make today will have an impact on tomorrow.

When I interviewed, I hated the question, "What do you see yourself doing five years from now?" Back then, I had no idea. Today, I have a different answer. Think.

I'm Here, Now What?

Complete the list below:
1. Five years from now you will be how old? Answer: _____.
2. Ten years from now I want to have the following skills:
   a. Be bilingual.
   b. Increased knowledge of computers and software.
   c. Increased knowledge of industry trends.
   d. Know two to three business people who impact my industry.
   e. Establish my upward-mobility plan.
   f. _____
   g. _____
   h. _____
3. My plan to achieve the skill includes:
   a. Researching the requirements by
      i. Talking to others who have attained what I desire.
      ii. Reading industry periodicals.
   b. Attending classes and workshops
   c. _____
   d. _____
   e. _____

Your list may extend beyond this page. Set a goal for yourself today because tomorrow is coming. What do you plan to do about it?

Passion

Passion cannot be put in a box for you to inspect. Passion is intangible. Passion exists within you even when others do not believe or see it.

Some of your successes come not from doing what's required, but from something in your spirit that makes it come easy. Passion. Discover and develop your inner drive.

My passions fall into three main categories: volunteering, public speaking and family. If you are trying to find your passion, then answer the following questions:

1. I love _____ so much that I would do it for free and without recognition.
2. If only I could do _____, I would feel more fulfilled in my career/life.
3. When I dream of my perfect career, I think about _____.
4. I need to complete _____ and _____ to reach my passion.
5. What barriers are keeping me from living out my passion?
6. What can I do to remove or neutralize the barriers?
7. Who can help me get to or live out my passion?
8. When do I plan to start seeking my passion?
9. When do I plan to start living my passion?

Passion is a flame that cannot be extinguished, no matter what the situation. Be realistic in your quest to find your passion. If your passion is to be an archeologist, then research the classes, degrees and experience needed. If your passion is to walk on the moon, then delve into NASA and astronomy. Investigate your passion by writing it, researching the idea and getting intelligent advice from your circle. Recognize your passion by the emotional stirring and realism in your plan.

Numerous books have been written about finding one's passion. Take your answers from the passion questions above and the dreaming answers from previous chapters to begin your passion-finding journey. Do not complicate your search. Spend time alone to think, pray and search inward. The power lies inside of you. The answers are there if you seek and acknowledge them.

When I moved away from my parents' home for the third and final time, I had a lot of time on my hands to be by myself. I was alone, but not lonely. During that time, I worshipped in different faiths, read books, thought and prayed. By spending time alone, I realized that one of my passions was speaking. I developed a one-woman play, *The Jazz in You*. I performed at local churches, nursing homes and service clubs and gave my all to complete strangers. Every time I finished, someone told me that I spoke directly to them.

Even now when I speak, I know I am going to talk to one person. The room may be filled with hundreds of people but I know I am there to help, educate or motivate one person. My passion to speak became a burning desire.

When I performed, I did not get paid. I did not do it for fame. I did it to reach that one person. A community can be changed for the better by one person. I have found my passion and look for ways to express it in my career, volunteer activities and with my family.

Since I found my passion, you can find yours. It may take some time, but it is possible. Do not give up. Search until you find it. We all have a spark and it must be kindled until the flame is visible to others. Only then will the light radiate for others to enjoy.

Enjoy the flame of others. Never blow out someone else's candle, so that yours will shine. Passion is a flame that helps light the world.

> *Nothing great in the world was ever accomplished without passion.*
> ~ Author Unknown.

Take steps — giant steps if you can —toward living your passion. If you lack the courage for giant steps, then take little ones. Either way, you will march toward the life of your dreams.

If we were to study successful women, I am sure we would find one consistent ingredient in their success recipe: passion. You may discover that you have several passions. You may find that some of them overlap. Your passion may change over time. Walking in your passion is the true secret to authenticity. Seek, discover and know your passions and you will come to know who you are.

Enjoy What You've Got

During one of my personnel reviews, I told my boss that I wanted to be the best director in the state and then I asked him what I needed to do to achieve it.

He said, "You are already the best. Now what you need to do is enjoy what you've got."

Betrayed. How could he say that I needed to enjoy what I had? He did not know what I had or did he? I had an epiphany that changed my life. I had a wonderful, supportive husband and a beautiful, loving family. I had fulfilling volunteer opportunities and a welcoming church family. I had plenty of opportunities to use my gifts. The list of what I had continued for a while. He was right. I had overlooked many blessings.

My perspective about my career has changed. I am good at what I do, but I have to put down the title of director and be me. You have reached the great plateau, when you realize that a job is what you do and not who you are.

The moment you think you have arrived may be the start of your departure. You will find yourself caught up in complacency that will yield nothing. No ideas. No growth.

Value who you are and what you bring to your career. Seek time for the things that you enjoy; especially the relationships in your life. Build on your strengths and start dreaming again.

I look at my grandmother's life as a reminder. She had a full life of work, church and travel. She lived in her own apartment and did what she wanted to do. The initial stages of dementia have affected her quality of life. She now lives with a roommate in a nursing home. Her vast clothing collection now fits inside one small closet. Decisions about her life are made by me, her power of attorney, and my mother, her only daughter.

Before my former boss told me that I was already the best director in the State of Ohio, I expected him to give me high-level advice, steps or observation. Could reaching the next level of career fulfillment be as simple as enjoying my current level of success? Could it be relaxing the self-imposed standards so I could measure up to my male peers? No matter how many awards I win, how many great reviews I get or how many people I help, I need to enjoy what I've got. Enjoy what you've got. From where I stand, I've got more than anyone else in the world.

I asked myself, "I'm here, now what?"

Only you can answer that question for you. With reflection, dreaming and self love, the answer will come. I am off to answer and fulfill the question for myself.

Until next time, enjoy.

I'm Here, Now What?

Quotes About or For Women

Women like silent men. They think they're listening.
~ Marcel Achard, Quote November 1956

Sure God created man before woman. But then you always make a rough draft before the final masterpiece.
~ Author Unknown.

Whatever women do they must do twice as well as men to be thought of half as good. Luckily, this is not difficult.
~ Charlotte Whitton

Women are always beautiful.
~ Villa Valo

Women get the last word in every argument. Anything a man says after that is the beginning of a new argument.
~ Author Unknown.

There is a special place in hell for women who do not help other women.
~ Madeline K. Albright

Women are like elephants to me. I like to look at them, but I wouldn't want to own one.
~ W.C. Fields

Women really do rule the world. They just haven't figured it out yet. When they do, and they will, we're all in big trouble.

~ Doctor Leon

I have an idea that the phrase "weaker sex" was coined by some woman to disarm some man she was preparing to overwhelm.
~ Ogden Nash

The torment that so many young women know, bound hand and foot by love and motherhood, without having forgotten their former dreams.
~ Simone de Beauvior

They call it PMS because Mad Cow Disease was already taken.
~ Author Unknown

You see, dear, it is true that woman was made from man's rib; she was really made from his funny bone.
~ J.M. Barrie, What Every Woman Knows

Women are never stronger than when they arm themselves with their weakness.
~ Marie de Vichy-Chamrond, Marquise Du Deffand, Letters to Voltaire

A woman should soften but not weaken a man.
~ Sigmund Freud

A woman wears her tears like jewelry.
~ Author Unknown

I'm Here, Now What?

I would rather trust a woman's instinct than a man's reason.
~ Stanley Baldwin Quotes

One is not born a woman, one becomes one.
~ Simone de Beauvior, the Second Sex 1949

It's the good girls who keep the diaries; the bad girls never have the time.
~ Tallulah Bankhead

I hate women because they always know where things are.
~ Voltaire

Toni Perry Gillispie

A Journal for Your Thoughts

About Toni Perry Gillispie

Toni Perry Gillispie is the director of external affairs at AT&T Ohio supporting several business units. She also manages the philanthropy, media relations and stakeholder relationships with the federal, state and city legislators and non-profits in nine Ohio counties.

Toni is a member of several boards and committees including the CityWide Development Corporation, YWCA Women of Influence, South Central Minority Business Certification, Dayton Urban League and chairwoman of Kids Voting – Dayton Region.

Her efforts in corporate and community have been acknowledged through numerous awards including the AT&T Supplier Diversity Advocate Award, the Dayton Chamber of Commerce Volunteer Award, the Ohio Hispanic Chamber Corporate Business Advocate Award, Top Ten Women 2007 Dayton Daily News, Top Ten Women African American CEO 2008 and the Dayton Business Journal 40 Under 40 Award.

Toni has a bachelor's degree in business administration from Wilberforce University and a master's degree in community economic development from Southern New Hampshire University. She is a certified economic development professional and an Advanced Toastmasters Bronze.

Toni enjoys volunteer activities, music, the arts and public speaking. She resides in Dayton, Ohio with her husband, Goodie, and their son.

Queen V Publishing
The Doorway to YOUR Destiny!

Go thou and publish abroad the kingdom of God.
—Luke 9:60

A Christian contract publisher committed to transforming manuscripts into polished works of art. **Queen V Publishing**, a company of standard and integrity, offers an alternative that allows God's word in YOU to do what it was sent to do for OTHERS.

Submit your manuscript online or by postal mail. Visit the website for complete guidelines and the contract plan that best fits your literary goals and needs.

QueenVPublishing.net

Valerie L. Coleman	Dr. Vivi Monroe Congress
Queen V Publishing	Queen V Publishing
Dayton, Ohio	Grand Prairie, Texas
937.307.0760	214.868.2016
Info@PenoftheWriter.com	LittleLightProd@aol.com

I'm Here, Now What?

Other Queen V Titles…

Patches of Inspiration™ – Harvesting Your Success
By Sonie Bigbee
ISBN-13: 978-0-9817436-2-2

PatchesofInspiration.com

Success is more than an idea or concept. Success is a living, tangible ingredient cultivated through the organic process of seeding, rooting and weeding.

In *Patches of Inspiration™ - Harvesting Your Success*, Sonie explains how to reap success by
- Seeding elements essential to fruitful living.
- Rooting factors you need to develop, deepen and grow
- Weeding, or complete removal, of obstacles that hinder growth.

With an inspirational approach to key areas in daily living, combined with biblical principles, you will learn how to seed, root and weed your way to success.

Pen of the Writer

*Out of Ephraim was there a root of them against Amalek; after thee, Benjamin, among thy people; out of Machir came down governors, and out of Zebulun they that handle the **pen of the writer**.*
~ Judges 5:14

P_{en} O_{f the} W_{rit}ER

A Christian publishing company committed to using the writing pen as a weapon to fight the enemy and celebrate the good news of Christ Jesus.

Taking writers from pen to paper to published!
Passionate Pens
Write On! Workshop
Pen to Paper Literary Symposium
Literary Management & Consultation

Pen of the Writer, LLC
Dayton, Ohio
937.307.0760
PenoftheWriter.com
info@PenoftheWriter.com

Manna for Mamma: Wisdom for Women in the Wilderness
By Dr. Vivi Monroe Congress
ISBN 13: 978-0-9748020-4-6

Manna for Mamma: Wisdom for Women in the Wilderness links the similarities between the Israelites' journey from captivity in Egypt toward freedom in the Promised Land of Canaan, and the ten most common experiences women face today during their personal pilgrimage: Beauty & Aging, Dating & Marriage, Education, Employment & Finances, Illness & Death, the Missing Man, Parenting, Position, Religion and Self-Esteem.

This book responds to the wilderness conditions in a woman's life by revealing that Jesus is her manna, available to both sustain and deliver her. *Manna for Mamma* will inspire women to move in the direction of His promises for her life, already fulfilled and awaiting her arrival.

"*Manna for Mamma* answers the hows and whys which come in those hard pressed, seasons of pruning and testing. Dr. Congress is bearing literary fruit to nourish us all!"
—Norma Jarrett, J.D., Author of *Sweet Magnolia*
(*Essence* Book Club Selection)

For information on bulk order purchasing or to schedule author appearance, visit
DrViviMonroeCongress.com and
MannaForMamma.com

Toni Perry Gillispie

Blended Families An Anthology
A Black Christian Book Distributors and Christian Small Publishers Association Bestseller!
By Valerie L. Coleman

ISBN-13: 978-0-9786066-0-2
With divorce, single-parent households and family crises on the rise, many people are experiencing the tumultuous dynamics of blended or stepfamilies. Learn biblical principles and practical tools to help your family thrive. ***Blended Families An Anthology*** ministers to the needs of those hurting and crying out for answers.

We are **not** the Brady Bunch!

Tainted Mirror An Anthology

By Valerie L. Coleman
ISBN: 978-0-9786066-1-9
What's keeping you from your destiny? Whether restricted by prison walls, the influence of others or held hostage by self-inflicted limitations, captivity starts in the mind. We allow our thoughts to create virtual restrainers that stifle our dreams and hinder our purpose.

Based on I Corinthians 13:12, ***Tainted Mirror An Anthology*** offers stories of hope and healing to overcome the mental, physical and emotional strongholds that keep us from fulfilling our destiny.

Available on **Amazon.com, BlackCBD.com** and **PenoftheWriter.com/Anthology**

I'm Here, Now What?

Order additional copies of

I'm Here, Now What?

The Inspired Word, LLC
PO Box 60096
Dayton, Ohio 45406
937.279.9545
TheInspiredWord.net
QueenVPublishing.net
ToniPerryGillispie@sbcglobal.net

* * * * * * * * * * * * * * * * * *

Please mail _____ copies of

I'm Here, Now What?

_____
Name

_____
Address

_____
City / State / Zip

(_____)_____
Phone

_____
Email

Quantity	Price Per Book	Total
	$9.95	
Sales Tax (Ohio residents add $0.70 per book)		
Shipping ($1.99 first book, $0.99 each add'l)		
Grand Total* (Payable to: Latonia Gillispie)		

* Certified check and money orders only

Toni Perry Gillispie

www.ingramcontent.com/pod-product-compliance
Lightning Source LLC
Chambersburg PA
CBHW071838290426
44109CB00017B/1848